THE GREAT EXCHANGE

Replacing Lies with Experiential Truth

Lillian M. Easterly-Smith, BCPC

*L*IFE*C*ARE
PUBLISHING

LifeCare Publishing is a branch of
LifeCare Christian Center
A non-profit faith-based ministry
www.LifeCareChristianCenter.org
info.lifecarecc@gmail.com
Westland, MI USA

Mission Statement
LifeCare Christian Center exists to partner with individuals, churches and the community in promoting spiritual, emotional, physical and relational wholeness, by providing quality, affordable care, education and training services from a Christian perspective.

CONTENTS

INTRODUCTION TO INNER HEALING PRAYER

Welcome to The Great Exchange inner healing prayer guide. I have put together this small booklet to provide support and guidance for the inner healing prayer process, for those who long to get the most out of personal inner healing prayer, and for those who are facilitating it with others.

The following verses provide the Biblical foundation for inner healing prayer.

The Great Exchange:

<u>Isaiah 61:1-3</u>

The Spirit of the Sovereign LORD is on me,
    because the LORD has anointed me
    to proclaim good news to the poor.
He has sent me to bind up the brokenhearted,
    to proclaim freedom for the captives
    and release from darkness for the prisoners,
[2] to proclaim the year of the LORD's favor
    and the day of vengeance of our God,

to comfort all who mourn,
³ and provide for those who grieve in Zion—
to bestow on them a crown of beauty
   instead of ashes,
the oil of joy
   instead of mourning,
and a garment of praise
   instead of a spirit of despair.
They will be called oaks of righteousness,
   a planting of the LORD
   for the display of his splendor.

Transformation/ Mind Renewal:

Romans 12:2
"Do not conform to the pattern of this world, but be transformed by the renewing of your mind. Then you will be able to test and approve what God's will is—his good, pleasing and perfect will."

Healing/ Freedom:

Psalm 107:19-20, NASB
"...they cried out to the Lord in their trouble; He saved them out of their distresses. He sent His Word and healed them, and delivered them from their destructions."

Much of what you will read and experience in these pages comes from a variety of sources and information that I have been exposed to over the years as it relates to inner healing. I have received mind renewal and healing as well as facilitated and trained/ coached individuals for thousands of hours during my many years of ministry. I believe these principles come directly from God, and if utilized, allow individuals to encounter and receive experiential truth from the Lord that transforms from the inside out.

Note: This booklet is best used in combination with the books mentioned at the end or as a tool after you have taken the basic training course which is where you will find all the Biblical support and deeper explanations of the process.

What is Inner Healing Prayer (IHP)?

IHP is all about mind renewal. God's Word tells us that we are "transformed by the renewing of our mind" (Romans 12:2). IHP is a process/ prayer time that a person can participate in so lies/ false beliefs can be exposed. Inner Healing Prayer is conversational prayer. It is communication to and from God that is specific to hurts in our past and false beliefs we have. Everyone has lies they believe. Everyone needs to have their minds renewed and lies replaced with truth. The lies we are discussing here come from events or possibly the "lack of good things" that happened or did not happen but were needed so that we might grow into maturity and live in truth. The enemy (Satan, the father of lies) uses these painful/ vulnerable experiences to set us up to internalize lies or falsely interpret what took place. If we believe lies, they may as well be the truth because every decision/ choice we make is always based upon what we believe. In those vulnerable moments in our past (oftentimes in childhood), we do not have the mental capacity or ability to experience a situation and analyze it properly. More often than not, everything is personalized, and therefore, we believe many self-lies that create negative self-talk which then leads to negative choices.

There are many types of lies, and I would encourage you to read *The Lies We Believe* by Dr. Chris Thurman to help you gain some understanding in this area, and also review Appendix I in this booklet which will be helpful in identifying categories of lies, the presenting emotion and possible belief statements.

Not all lies/ false beliefs come from childhood. There are times when we get negative imprints in our minds because of situations as an adult as well (i.e., crisis situations, unexpected death & tragedy, divorce, etc.). Every painful event can be used by the enemy of our souls (the father of lies) to deceive us and get us to believe lies. However, "greater is He that is in us than he that is in the world", therefore, we can take heart! This prayer time can be the opportunity you have been looking for to finally embrace truth and walk in peace and freedom!

Who Needs It?

Everyone Needs Healing and Mind Renewal

Most people have not suffered a severe trauma, but everyone has been wounded at some level – all of us have memories that are imbedded with lies. When we experientially "know" God in these places and receive His truth, we will find His rest, joy and peace. Paul said, "I pray that the *eyes of your heart* may be enlightened, so that you will *know* what is the hope of His calling, what are the riches of the glory of His inheritance in the saints." (Eph. 1:18, NASB, emphasis added). As the "eyes of our heart" are opened, we will see who we are in Christ and come to *"know"* the love of Christ experientially (not just with our head but with our heart).

When anyone experiences the presence of Christ, there is always miraculous change/ transformation. This prayer process is not about having an "emotional experience." We are not chasing after emotional experiences. Anyone can have an emotional experience at a music concert or a sporting event or even a church service. Spiritual moments that are experiential—when we have an encounter with Jesus, are moments when we are changed; that is what inner healing prayer is about. So, yes, everyone can benefit from inner healing prayer.

Basic Principles of Inner Healing Prayer (IHP)

1. My present situation is rarely the primary source of my pain.

2. If I try to resolve my current conflict without finding healing for my past wounds, I will, at best, only find temporary relief. However, if my past is healed, my present can be redeemed.

3. The emotions I currently feel are most often "echoes" of my past that can be used as a bridge to the wounds in my life.

4. I must let go the present situation and release it of being the primary source of my pain.

5. If I refuse to feel, I ultimately cannot heal. I must choose to look at my past and the wounds I have face to face, feeling them fully once again.

6. There are three things necessary for inner healing:

   - the emotional historical "echo" from the past

   - a memory picture or thought

   - the belief I have in that place (the lie)

7. The emotional pain I have in the memory comes predominantly from the interpretation of the event (the lie).

8. The emotional pain I feel will match the lies I believe.

9. If I believe a lie, it may as well be the truth because the consequences and choices I make will be the same.

10. To be free of my false beliefs will require me to embrace and confess the lie rather than reject or denounce it.

11. In the midst of my pain and darkness, I will come to realize the debilitating grip this belief has on my life.

12. It is in this state of helplessness, and oftentimes, hopelessness, that I am able to receive healing and truth from God. When the way is made clear for me to receive, God speaks in whatever way He chooses (a picture, His still small voice, His peace, etc.). His truth/ His communication to me, sets me free of the lie I believe in that place. I will be free at last!

CHAPTER 1

PREPARATION FOR PRAYER TIME

In Appendix III you will find a confidential personal inventory. If you have never had any form of counseling, inner healing or support group experience, I encourage you to take the time to do this introspective inventory that will help you gain insight into your life experiences. The inventory is quite extensive, so do not feel you must complete it in one sitting. Once you have finished, make a decision to set aside some quiet, uninterrupted time with God for your first inner healing prayer experience. I recommend at least two hours so you have plenty of time to pray and then have some processing/ reflective time and journaling afterward.

CHAPTER 2

GUIDE FOR
INNER HEALING PRAYER

S tart your prayer time with something like:

Father, I thank You that You are the God of truth. You desire for me to have the ability to walk in the truth and so I come to You today asking You to guide me into the truth during this time with You. I ask that You give me the strength and courage to face anything I need to face, feel, remember or sense. I thank You for Your protection from the evil one during this time and ask that every thought, image, feeling or memory be only according to Your plan and purpose—Your divine purpose. Give me the ability to keep moving forward, trusting that You will give me all I need to gain the insight and understanding necessary to expose my false beliefs and get to a place of peace and truth as the Holy Spirit leads. In Jesus' Name, Amen.

Keeping your eyes closed during the prayer time is recommended but not necessary. I find it much easier to keep from distractions when eyes are closed. Also, as you consider the events/ situations God would have you deal with in a session, a helpful tool is to put a dollar amount on the event that will give you indication of the possibility of a lie being present. If we give a $5 event, $500 worth of emotion, that is a good place to start as the proportion of the emotion given the event will be the bridge to the false belief/ lie that the Lord wants exposed.

1. Scan your emotions and your whole being. Is there anything that's not at peace, feels unsettled/ uncomfortable? If so, what is it? If there is nothing currently present, take a few moments to scan over the last several weeks – is there an event that stands out that gives you strong, unpleasant emotion?

_____

_____

_____

_____

_____

2. Describe what you're feeling.

_____

_____

_____

_____

_____

3. Ask yourself, "Where have I felt this way before?" Mentally and emotionally engage in that thought. Consider any words, memories, or pictures that come to mind. If writing it down will help, you may want to do so.

_____

_____

_____

_____

4. As you look at that picture, memory or consider that thought, how did you feel in that place?

    _____
    _____
    _____
    _____
    _____

5. Ask yourself, "What did I internalize about this?" "What do I believe in this place?" If at any time you get stuck, don't hesitate to ask God to help give you courage to face what you need to face, feel what you need to feel, and to move forward.

    _____
    _____
    _____
    _____
    _____

6. Once the belief is exposed, ask God what His perspective is. What does He see? What is the Truth He wants you to know? Write down what you hear, sense or anything that comes to mind—a picture, memory, song, scripture verse, words, etc. _____
    _____
    _____
    _____
    _____

7. If you do not hear, see, sense, or get to the Truth, ask yourself if there is another place where you felt/ experienced the same emotion or thoughts. Keep processing as each memory, picture, thought comes to mind – going back through steps #3-6.

8. Look back at your initial feelings and the circumstances surrounding them. Now, with this Truth, how do you feel in those circumstances? You may need to go back to step 2 and follow through with more feelings until you experience peace. If a lack of peace is truth-based* (sadness, righteous anger), you can release these feelings to God as He leads.

_____

_____

_____

_____

_____

*Note: Truth-based emotions are the feelings we have that exist because of a truthful conclusion. Everyone has pain and anger related to victimization or an offense. And let's face it, we have all been victimized or offended in various ways. However, what we do with those emotions can lead to destruction. God provides another way – we do not need to carry them. The Apostle Peter tells us under the inspiration of the Holy Spirit to …cast our cares/ anxieties upon Him because He cares for us (see 1 Peter 5:6-8). We can define those cares as worry, fear, anxiety, anger, hatred, sadness, etc. Jesus is willing to receive your truth-based emotion; you can release it to Him. It may or may not be in the current inner healing session as there are times when we have not allowed ourselves to process grief and anger and therefore, He will allow us to experience it for some time to expand our hearts for empathy, compassion, love and deep understanding of others. Do not make attempts at rushing the process; listen for His leading.

Guide for Inner Healing Prayer – EXAMPLE 1

1. Scan your emotions and your whole being. Is there anything that's not at peace, feels unsettled/ uncomfortable? If so, what is it? If there is nothing currently present, take a few moments to scan over the last several weeks – is there an event that stands out that gives you strong, unpleasant emotion?

   _____Yes. Uncomfortable working outside._____

2. Describe what you're feeling.

   _____Anxiety; fear of being stung._____

3. Ask yourself, "Where have I felt this way before?" Mentally and emotionally engage in that thought. Consider any words, memories, or pictures that come to mind. If writing it down will help, you may want to do so.

   _____I almost died from an anaphylactic reaction to a bee sting recently._____

4. As you look at that picture, memory or consider that thought, how did you feel in that place?

   _____Mostly peaceful and secure, but aware of how close I was to death._____

5. Ask yourself, "What did I internalize about this?" "What do I believe in this place?" If at any time you get stuck, don't hesitate to ask God to help give you courage to face what you need to face, feel what you need to feel, and to move forward.

   _____I believe I can die before God's time for me depending on my choices in working outside._____

6. Once the belief is exposed, ask God what His perspective is. What does He see? What is the Truth He wants you to know? Write down what you hear, sense or anything that comes to mind—a picture, memory, song, scripture verse, words, etc. <u>"I was in it with you the whole time, in control, sustaining your life; I wasn't allowing anything that I wouldn't use for good. I brought your husband home at just the right time. I worked out all the details to conform it to My plan. Satan means these things for evil; I use them for good."</u>

7. If you do not hear, see, sense, or get to the Truth, ask yourself if there is another place where you felt/ experienced the same emotion or thoughts. Keep processing as each memory, picture, thought comes to mind – going back through steps #3-6.

8. Look back at your initial feelings and the circumstances surrounding them. Now, with this Truth, how do you feel in those circumstances? You may need to go back to step 2 and follow through with more feelings until you experience peace. If a lack of peace is *truth-based (sadness, righteous anger), you can release these feelings to God as He leads.

<u>More peaceful with working outside knowing that my circumstances are in God's control and He won't allow anything that He can't use for good.</u>

Guide for Inner Healing Prayer – EXAMPLE 2

1. Scan your emotions and your whole being. Is there anything that's not at peace, feels unsettled/uncomfortable? If so, what is it? If there is nothing currently present, take a few moments to scan over the last several weeks – is there an event that stands out that gives you strong, unpleasant emotion?

   Anxiousness at no longer being the go to person at work, feeling replaced. Outside of my control. Feeling the same way in a couple friendships as well. Loss because I am no longer in a certain inner circle that I once was.

2. Describe what you're feeling.

   Loneliness, anxious, unrest, out of control. Desiring to be on someone's "it" list.

3. Ask yourself, "Where have I felt this way before?" Mentally and emotionally engage in that thought. Consider any words, memories, or pictures that come to mind. If writing it down will help, you may want to do so.

   Memory in the car where my Dad is choosing his new step children over me.

4. As you look at that picture, memory or consider that thought, how did you feel in that place?

   Alone, left behind.

5. Ask yourself, "What did I internalize about this?" "What do I believe in this place?" If at any time you get stuck, don't hesitate to ask God to help give you

courage to face what you need to face, feel what you need to feel, and to move forward.

I am not worth keeping. I am replaceable. I know for sure as a small child, my earthly father loved me very much – I was Daddy's girl. I also know and believe that God the Father loves me immeasurably. Therefore, if my earthly father who loved me so much can replace me (I am no longer Daddy's girl), then my Godly father can as well - which means I can't trust or rely on God. God's feelings will change just like my earthly father's did.

6. Once the belief is exposed, ask God what His perspective is. What does He see? What is the Truth He wants you to know? Write down what you hear, sense or anything that comes to mind—a picture, memory, song, scripture verse, words, etc.

a. He is showing me all the endless ways He has continued to pursue me for decades. Over and over and over, even though I was at times pushing him away.

b. This is the complete opposite of what my earthly father did.....I never got birthday cards, I never got phone calls......it was as if I didn't exist anymore.

c. God is showing me how he kept me next to Him my whole life. Saying "I can't live without you!"

d. He says "Not only can I NOT forget you....I can't live without you."

e. He pursues me, and pursues me, and pursues me. Never forgetting, never leaving my side.

7. If you do not hear, see, sense, get to the Truth, ask yourself if there is another place where you felt/ experienced the same emotion or thoughts. Keep processing as each memory, picture, thought comes to mind – going back through steps #3-6.

8. Look back at your initial feelings and the circumstances surrounding them. Now, with this Truth, how do you feel in those circumstances? You may need to go back to step 2 and follow through with more feelings until you experience peace. If a lack of peace is *truth-based (sadness, righteous anger), you can release these feelings to God as He leads.

   Peace. _____

CHAPTER 3

WHAT HAPPENS IF NOTHING HAPPENS?

Possible Hindrances & Next Steps

D o not be discouraged if the Lord does not reveal truth or you feel stuck or do not find immediate release. It is not because God is withholding or that the process is not working. There are several reasons this happens; following are possibilities:

> ➤ Original lie not identified

> ➤ Demonic interference

> ➤ Logical thinking

> ➤ Unconfessed sin

> ➤ Disassociation

> ➤ Revengeful emotions such as anger, hate, rage, resentment

➢ Difficulty identifying the emotion or false belief: (If you are having difficulty verbalizing or connecting with the emotion or false belief, reading through the Lie/ Emotional Identification Sheet [Appendix I] may be of help to you. I have also included in Appendix II a list of questions that may be helpful in making better connections.)

As you can see, there is a variety of reasons why a session does not go as you would like. Rather than attempting to address all the hindrances in this booklet or explain all the options available to remove the hindrances, I would like to recommend that you reach out to someone in the area that is familiar with this process. Sometimes, God intentionally will not allow us to get to a place of truth without someone else being involved. I suspect a variety of different reasons for this, two of which are breaking pride and healing shame. There are also times when we cannot seem to get to the false beliefs because it is just too emotional. We cannot seem to hear or figure out where to go next because the feelings are overwhelming. Again, reach out. There are others in the Body of Christ ready and willing to help you. We all need each other.

Where do I go for help?

Feel free to start by contacting our organization. We are familiar with area churches and ministries that are partnering with us to help individuals grow into wholeness through inner healing prayer and other God-directed methods.

www.lifecarechristiancenter.org

Email: Info.LifeCareCC@gmail.com   734.629.3551

Recommended Reading:

Healing Life's Hurts – Edward Smith

Emotionally Healthy Spirituality – Peter Scazzero

Victory over the Darkness – Neil Anderson

LIE/ EMOTIONAL IDENTIFICATION SHEET

Category	Possible Lies Producing Emotions
Abandonment	"I am all alone. I have been overlooked. I will always be alone. They do not need me. I don't matter. No one even cares. They are not coming back. There is no one to protect me. God has forsaken me. No one will believe me. I cannot trust anyone. I am afraid they won't come back."
Shame	"I am so stupid, ignorant, an idiot. I should have done something to have stopped it from happening. I allowed it. I was a participant. I should have known better. It was my fault. I should have told someone. I knew what was going to happen yet I stayed anyway.

I felt pleasure so I must have wanted it. I was a participant. It happened because of my looks, my gender, my body, etc. I should have stopped them. I did not try to run away. I deserved it. I am cheap like a slut. I was paid for service rendered. I kept going back. I did it to him/her first. I am bad, dirty, shameful, sick, nasty."

Fear

"I am going to die, he/she is going to hurt me. I do not know what to do. If I tell they will come back and hurt me. If I trust, I will die. He/she/they are coming back. It is just a matter of time before it happens again. If I let him/her/them into my life they will hurt me too. Something bad will happen. If I tell, stop it, confront it, they are going to get me. Doom is just around the corner."

Powerlessness/ Trapped

"I cannot stop this. He/she/they are too strong to resist."

There is no way out

"I am too weak to resist. The pain is too great to bear. I cannot get away. I'm going to die and I cannot do anything about it. I cannot get loose. I am overwhelmed. I don't know what to do. Everything is out of control. I am pulled from every direction. Not even God can help me. I am too small to do anything."

Tainted

"I am dirty, shameful, evil, perverted, etc. because of what happened to me. My life is ruined. I will never feel clean again. Everyone can see my shame, filth, dirtiness, etc. I will always be hurt/damaged, broken because of what happened. I will never be happy. I will always be unclean, filthy, etc. God could never want me after what has happened to me. My body parts are dirty. No one will ever really be able to love me."

Invalidation

"I am not loved, needed, wanted, cared for, or important. They do not need me. I am worthless; I have no value. I am unimportant. I was a mistake. I should have never been born. I am in the way. I am a burden. I was never liked by them because I was _____. God could never love me or accept me. I could never be as _____ as she/he. I could never jump high enough to please him/her. I am not acceptable."

Hopeless

"It is never going to get any better. There is no way out. It will just happen again and again. There is no good thing for me. I have no reason to live. There are no options for me. I just want to die. Nothing good will ever come of this."

Confusion

"I don't know what is happening to me. Everything is confusing. This does not make any sense. Why would they do this to me?" (This lie is sometimes confused with demonic interference. Demons will cause confusion in a memory which will feel much like a confusion lie.) Can't verbalize—sometimes this is due to the fact that the memory coming forward is very early—before 2 yrs. old.

This section on possible lies provided from material presented by Dr. Ed Smith from a handout given in one of his seminars.

HELPFUL QUESTIONS TO USE DURING THE PRAYER TIME

Other than those already listed in the Guide and Examples given, the following may be helpful if you seem to be stuck or unsure where to go next, whether you are doing a session on yourself or facilitating someone else. Remember you and every person you work with has the choice to move forward or not.

"Why are you_____about moving forward/ going to the memory? What do you believe will happen if you do?"

Look inside and see if you can discover what your mind is doing to block your progress. See if you can figure out what is happening inside to block the pain (the wall, lack of emotion, creating the headache, sleepiness, etc.). "If these protective devices were not present, what do you believe will happen?"

If anger is present: "What do you believe that anger is doing for you? What will happen if it is no longer present? What is the Lord asking you to do with it right now?"

"What do you believe will happen if you go to the place where you first felt this shame/ guilt? What is keeping you from feeling/ getting to the source of your shame? Are you willing to allow the Lord to give you courage to get there?"

"When you think about moving toward the source of the pain, do you feel any resistance or hesitancy?" "Is there some part of your thinking that is not letting you see, feel or remember? What do you believe will happen if you do?"

Questions for Truth based emotions or conclusions you come to:

Examples:

"What does it feel like to know that _____ never (loved, accepted, valued) you?"

"Because you believe _____ never (loved, accepted, valued) you causes you to believe what about you?"

(Note: You can use similar questions in situations where a person feels rejected or abandoned.)

Feel the feelings then ask: "Because _____ (rejected, abandoned, intentionally hurt/ wounded) you, you believe what about yourself in that place?"

There will be points as you go through these questions that you simply stop and listen allowing the Lord to speak in whatever way He chooses in response.

PERSONAL INVENTORY

Family History

A. Religious

1. To your knowledge, have any of your parents, grandparents or great-grandparents ever been involved in any occult, cultic or non-Christian religious practices? Please Describe.

2. Briefly describe your parents' Christian experience (i.e., If they were believers, did they profess and live their Christianity?).

B. Marital Status

1. Are your parents presently married or divorced? Describe their relationship.

2. Was your father dominating/controlling? Explain.

   Was your mother? Explain:

3. How did your father treat your mother?

4. To your knowledge, was there ever an adulterous affair in your parents' or grandparents' relationships? Any incestuous relationships?

5. Were you adopted or raised by foster parents or legal guardians?

C. Sibling Data
   1. Sex and age of your sibling(s) and place yourself in the birth order.

2. Describe the emotional atmosphere in your home while you were growing up. Include a brief description of your relationship with your parents and sibling(s).

D. Health
   1. Are there any addiction problems in your family history (alcohol, drugs, etc.)? Describe:

   2. Is there any history of mental illness? Describe.

   3. Indicate if you have any history of the following recurring ailments in your family:
      ☐ Tuberculosis
      ☐ Cancer
      ☐ Heart disease
      ☐ Ulcers
      ☐ Diabetes
      ☐ Glandular problems
      ☐ Other

   4. How would you describe your family's concern for:
      a. Diet:

b. Exercise:

c. Rest:

E. Moral Climate
   1. In each category, describe the moral atmosphere in which you were raised during the first 18 years of your life:

   Clothing

   Sex

   Dating

   Movies

   Music

   Literature

   Free will

   Drinking

   Smoking

   Church attendance

History of Personal Health

A. Physical

1. Describe your eating habits.
   Do you lean toward eating only junk food or only eating healthy food?
   Do you eat regularly or sporadically?
   Is your diet balanced; etc.?

2. Do you have any addictions or cravings that cause you difficulty in controlling your intake of sweets, drugs, alcohol, or food in general? Explain.

3. Do you have any problems sleeping? Are you having any recurring nightmares or other sleep disturbances? Describe:

4. Does your schedule allow for regular periods of rest and relaxation?

5. Have you ever experienced any type of trauma (i.e., history of abuse: physical, emotional, or sexual; involvement in a severe accident; death of family member; etc.)? Explain.

B. Mental
   1. Describe your earliest memory.

   2. Do you have periods or blocks of time in your past that you can't remember? Describe.

3. Indicate any of the following which you have or are presently struggling with:
   - [ ] daydreaming
   - [ ] lustful thoughts
   - [ ] inferiority
   - [ ] worry
   - [ ] doubts
   - [ ] fantasizing
   - [ ] obsessive thoughts
   - [ ] insecurity
   - [ ] dizziness
   - [ ] headaches
   - [ ] compulsive thoughts
   - [ ] inadequacy
   - [ ] blasphemous thoughts

4. How many hours of TV do you watch per week?

   What programs are you drawn to?

5. How many hours do you spend a week reading?

   What do you primarily read (newspaper, magazines, books, etc.) and on what topics?

6. How much time do you spend listening to music?

What type of music do you listen to?

7. Would you consider yourself to be an optimist or a pessimist (i.e., do you have a tendency to see the good in people and life, or the bad)?

8. Do you have regular devotions, Bible reading, prayer?

C. Emotional
1. Indicate which of the following emotions you are presently having difficulty controlling:
   ☐ frustration
   ☐ anger
   ☐ anxiety
   ☐ loneliness
   ☐ worthlessness
   ☐ depression
   ☐ hatred
   ☐ bitterness
   ☐ fear of dying
   ☐ fear of losing your mind
   ☐ fear of committing suicide
   ☐ fear of hurting loved ones

☐ fear of going to hell
☐ fear of abandonment
☐ fear of _____

2. Which of the above listed emotions do you feel are sinful? Why?

3. Concerning your emotions, whether positive or negative, please indicate which of the following best describes you:

☐ readily express my emotions
☐ express some of my emotions, but not all
☐ readily acknowledge their presence, but reserved in expressing them
☐ tendency to suppress my emotions
☐ find it safest not to express how I feel
☐ tendency to disregard how I feel since I cannot trust my feelings
☐ consciously or subconsciously deny them since it is too painful to deal with them

4. Is there someone in your life with whom you could be emotionally honest right now (i.e., you could tell this person exactly how you feel about yourself, life and other people)? List them:

5. How important is it that we are emotionally honest before God, and do you feel that you are? Explain.

D. Spiritual History
   1. Suppose you died tonight and appeared before God in Heaven and He were to ask you "By what right should I allow you into my presence?" How would you answer Him?

   2. Are you plagued with doubts concerning your salvation? Please explain.

   3. Are you presently enjoying fellowship with other believers and, if so, where and when?

   4. Are you under authority of a local church where the Bible is preached, and do you regularly support it with your time, talent and treasure? If not, why?

Non-Christian Spiritual Experience Inventory

Indicate any of the following with which you or your ancestors have had any involvement. Indicate those in which you have participated, whether for fun, out of curiosity or in earnest.

- ☐ Psychic readings
- ☐ Christian Science
- ☐ Card laying
- ☐ Unity
- ☐ Crystal ball
- ☐ The Way International
- ☐ Palm reading
- ☐ Unification Church
- ☐ Tea leaves
- ☐ Mormonism
- ☐ Tarot cards
- ☐ Church of the Living World
- ☐ Attended or participated in a séance
- ☐ The Local Church
- ☐ Attended in or participated in a spiritualist meeting
- ☐ World Wide Church of God (H.W. Armstrong)
- ☐ Ouija board
- ☐ Children of God
- ☐ Magic Eight Ball
- ☐ Jehovah Witnesses
- ☐ Automatic (spirit writing)
- ☐ Unitarianism
- ☐ Levitation

- ☐ Masonic Orders
- ☐ Table lifting
- ☐ Read or followed the Horoscopes
- ☐ Zen Buddhism
- ☐ Astrology
- ☐ Hare Krishna
- ☐ Clairvoyance
- ☐ Baha'ism
- ☐ Telepathy
- ☐ Rosicrucian
- ☐ ESP
- ☐ New Age
- ☐ Speaking in a trance
- ☐ Inner Peace movement
- ☐ Mystical Meditation
- ☐ Spiritual Frontiers Fellowship
- ☐ Astral Projection/Travel
- ☐ Transcendental Meditation
- ☐ Magical Charming
- ☐ EST/The Forum
- ☐ Fetishism (objects of worship/idols)
- ☐ Eckankar
- ☐ Cabala /Kabala
- ☐ Mind control philosophies
- ☐ Materialization
- ☐ Science of the Mind
- ☐ Metaphysics
- ☐ Science of Creative Intelligence
- ☐ Self realization
- ☐ Theosophical Society
- ☐ Witchcraft
- ☐ Islam

- ☐ Sorcery
- ☐ Black Muslim
- ☐ Mental Suggestion
- ☐ Hinduism
- ☐ Dream Interpretation
- ☐ I Ching
- ☐ Being hypnotized
- ☐ Practiced self-hypnosis
- ☐ Practiced Eastern religion while participating in yoga
- ☐ Practiced Water/Witching (dowsing) rod /pendulum
- ☐ Other_____

Have you ever…..

- ☐ Had a spirit guide?
- ☐ Read or possessed occult literature, especially the Satanic Bible, Book of Shadows, Sixth and Seventh Books of Moses?
- ☐ Read or studied parapsychology?
- ☐ Practiced black or white magic?
- ☐ Possessed occult or pagan religious objects which were made for use in pagan temples or religious rites or in the practice of magic, sorcery, witchcraft, divination or spiritualism?
- ☐ Seen or been involved in Satan worship?
- ☐ Sought healing (either as a child or as an adult) through magic conjuration, charming, psychic healing or New Age medicine?
- ☐ Tried to locate a missing person or object by consulting someone with psychic powers?

☐ Encountered ghosts or materializations of persons known to be dead?

☐ Entered into a blood pact with another person?

☐ Been involved with heavy metal or allied kinds of rock music with a satanic/ angry message?

☐ Heard voices in your mind or had compulsive thoughts that were foreign to what you believe?

☐ Had periods in childhood or the present when you cannot remember what happened?

☐ Have you ever attended a New Age or parapsychology seminar, or consulted a medium, spiritist or channeler? Explain:

☐ Do you or have you ever had an imaginary friend or spirit guide offering you guidance or companionship? Explain:

☐ Have you ever heard voices in your mind or had repeating and nagging thoughts that were foreign to what you believe or feel, like there was a dialogue going on in your head? Explain:

What other spiritual experiences have you had that would be considered out of the ordinary such as sensing an evil presence in your room at night as a child?

Have you been a victim of any form of spiritual abuse? Explain:

Once you have completed the personal inventory take some time to go through a life/ historical timeline. This can be done in sections and you may want to spread it out over several days/ weeks.

This section, "Non-Christian Spiritual Experience Inventory", provided from material presented by Neil Anderson in a booklet entitled "Steps to Freedom".

Historical Timeline:

Take five year sections of your life and jot down any significant memories or events that come to mind regarding that time period, and then jot down the presenting emotion it creates. Include all events that come to mind – positive and negative.

1-5 years of age

5-10 years of age

10-15 years of age

15-20 years of age

20-25 years of age

25-30 years of age

Etc.

This exercise will be very helpful as you go through the healing/ growth process.

REFERENCES

"Non-Christian Spiritual Experience Inventory" in Appendix III is from a booklet called the *Steps to Freedom* by Neil Anderson, Freedom In Christ Ministries.

The list of possible lies in Appendix I came from Dr. Ed Smith from a handout given in one of his seminars.

CONTACT INFORMATION

LifeCare Christian Center

www.LifeCareChristianCenter.org

Email: Info.LifeCareCC@gmail.com

Facebook: https://www.facebook.com/LifeCareCC

Phone: 734.629.3551